HOW DO I BECOME AN . . . ?

EMS Worker

Mindi Rose Englart

Photographs by Peter Casolino

**BLACKBIRCH®
PRESS**

THOMSON

GALE

San Diego • Detroit • New York • San Francisco • Cleveland • New Haven, Conn. • Waterville, Maine • London • Munich

THOMSON

GALE

For more information, contact
The Gale Group, Inc.
27500 Drake Rd.
Farmington Hills, MI 48331-3535
Or you can visit our Internet site at http://www.gale.com

Photo Credits: Cover, all photos © Peter Casolino; pages 14, 16 © PhotoDisc; page 17 © Bruce Glassman

LIBRARY OF CONGRESS CATALOGING-IN-PUBLICATION DATA

Englart, Mindi.
  EMS Worker/ by Mindi Rose Englart.
    p. cm. — (How do I become a: series)
Includes index.
  ISBN 1-56711-420-2
  1. Emergency medical technicians—Vocational guidance-Juvenile literature.
  I. Title. II. Series.
  RA645.5 .E545 2003   2002007277

Printed in China
10 9 8 7 6 5 4 3 2 1

CONTENTS

Dedication
To my mom, Carol Englart

Special Thanks
The publisher and the author would like to thank Adam Rinko, Paul Brooks, and AMR for their generous help putting this project together. If you would like more information about the company featured in this book, visit the AMR web site at www. amr-inc.com.

People who work in Emergency Medical Services (EMS) are an important part of health care in the United States. They are often the first to offer medical help in an emergency. Across the country, EMS workers save hundreds of lives every day. How does someone become an EMS worker?

An EMS Worker is often the first person to offer medical help in an emergency. ▶

Emergency Medical Services

EMS workers help victims in medical emergencies, such as when people have heart attacks. EMS workers' main job is to help patients who are injured or sick. They must also get patients who need more help safely to a hospital.

EMS workers have to stay calm while they work. They need to be able to get people to do what they ask. EMS workers are also brave. Sometimes they risk their lives to help others.

There are two types of EMS workers: Emergency Medical Technicians (EMTs) and paramedics. They both have the same training up to a certain point. After that, trainees must take more classes to become paramedics.

One difference between paramedics and EMTs is that paramedics are able to give medicine to patients—EMTs are not. EMTs and paramedics both work with police and fire departments—sometimes even the FBI!

An EMT can give basic medical care to a victim— but he or she cannot give out medicine.

American Medical Response (AMR) is a company that hires EMS workers. AMR is the largest private ambulance business in the United States. They have more than 19,000 employees in 35 states. They help about 4 million patients every year. AMR even operates 911. People call 911 when they need help in an emergency. AMR lets people who are interested in EMS careers ride with one of their ambulance crews.

▲ AMR in New Haven, Connecticut, is the largest private ambulance business in the United States.

An EMS teacher talks to a class. People who want to become EMTs must take 130 hours of training.

About 50% of EMS professionals begin training when they are in high school.

EMS Training

People who want EMT careers must take 130 hours of training. They can begin training at the age of 15 1/2. Students take classes at colleges and special EMS training centers. This training teaches students the basic medical skills they will need to work on an ambulance crew.

EMTs learn to give advanced first aid. They give oxygen to people who have trouble breathing. They learn how to use bandages to stop bleeding. They also learn how to keep broken bones from moving.

Learning to Know What Is Wrong with a Patient

EMS workers usually see a patient before doctors do. This is because they get to the scene first. EMS workers must learn to take care of life-threatening problems. They are taught how to get patients ready to be moved to a hospital.

EMT students learn how to carefully look at a patient. They must quickly decide what is wrong. There may be more than one problem. For example, a victim who has been in a car accident may have broken bones and a head injury. EMT students learn to tell which problem is more serious.

EMT students practice first aid on life-like dummies. Students learn to "look, listen, and feel" to see if a patient is breathing. They look to see if a person's chest rises and falls. They listen to hear if a victim is breathing. And they feel to see if air comes out of a patient's nose and mouth.

A student looks, ▶
listens, and feels.

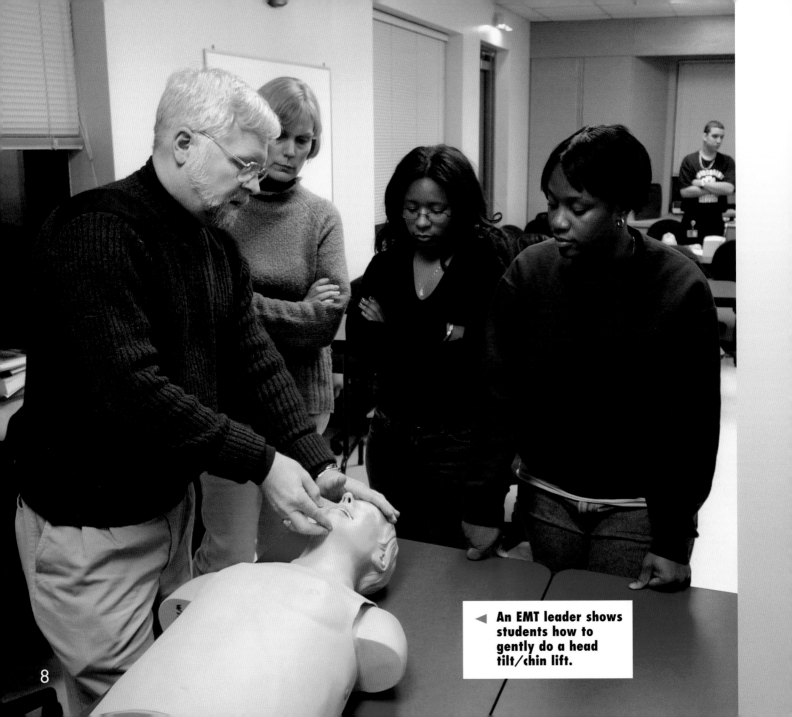

An EMT leader shows students how to gently do a head tilt/chin lift.

8

Creating an Airway

EMTs must know how to help a patient who cannot breathe. A person's airway is his or her mouth and throat. If a person's airway is blocked, he or she will be unable to breathe.

Students learn how to do a head tilt/chin lift. They gently move a patient's head back. This will open up an airway in the throat—unless there is an object stuck in it. EMTs move their fingers through a patient's mouth. They do this to check for objects that may be blocking the patient's airway. Even a tongue can block an airway. This is common if a victim has seizures (a sudden loss of body control) or passes out. EMT students learn to use a clear plastic tube to clear a patient's throat. This also prevents the tongue from blocking a victim's airway.

A leader has students practice a chin lift on themselves. ▼

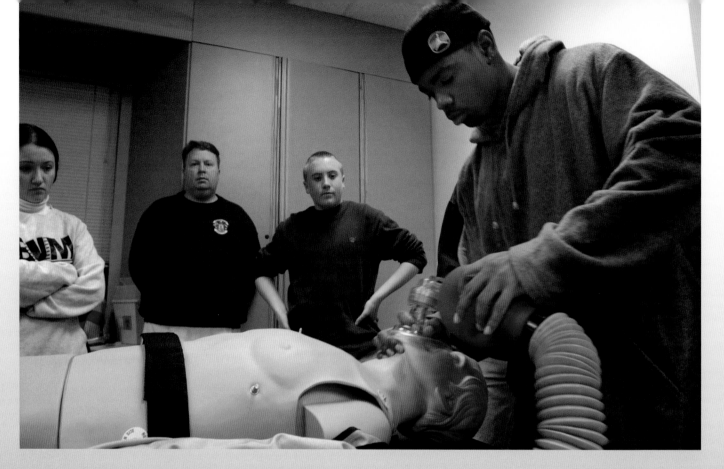

A student practices ▲
with an oxygen
mask on a dummy.

CPR

EMTs learn how to do a lifesaving procedure called CPR
on a patient whose heart and lungs have stopped working.
Emergency workers use CPR on a patient to get blood and
oxygen to the rest of his or her body. EMTs are taught how
to breathe for the victim. They blow air into the victim' s
mouth to get oxygen into his or her lungs.

They must also press on a patient's chest in a certain way. This makes the heart pump again. In CPR class, EMT students learn to use special masks and pumps. These tools help get air into the lungs. Students learn to do CPR on adults, children, and even babies.

After a heart attack, a heart can shake uncontrollably. Because it does not beat, it pumps no blood. Students learn how to use an AED machine. This machine shocks a patient's heart. An AED is supposed to return a heart to its normal beat. If a patient's heart is badly damaged, the machine may not work.

CPR doubles a person's chance of survival after a heart attack.

An EMT student practices using a special mask and pump on an infant model.

11

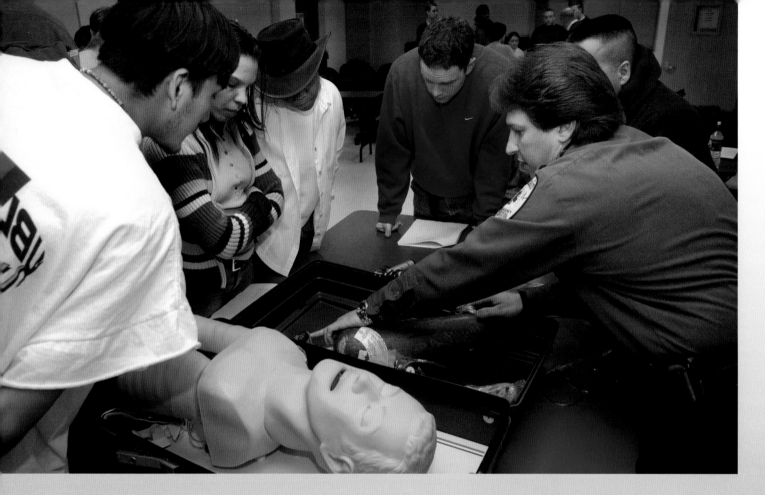

Oxygen Therapy

Oxygen is one of the most common aids EMS workers give
to patients. Patients may need oxygen during an asthma attack,
a heart attack, or after they've been in a fire. Any of these common
problems can stop people from breathing. Brain damage or death
can occur in less than eight minutes without oxygen.

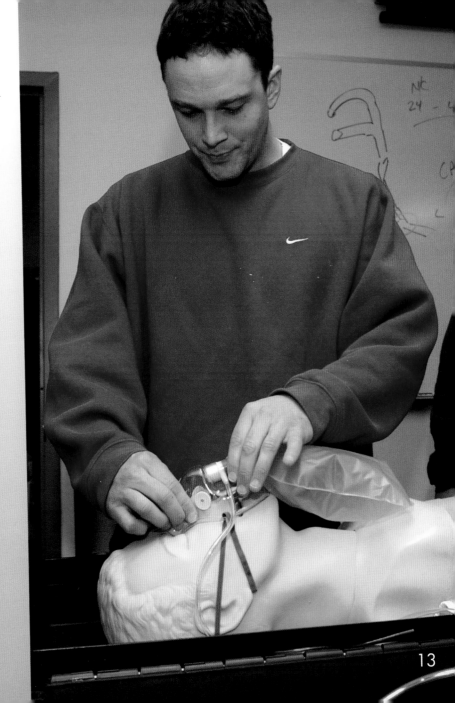

Students learn to use oxygen tanks to give the right amount of oxygen to patients. Sometimes oxygen is given through a mask. When victims cough a lot, EMTs insert breathing tubes in patients' noses. This helps patients inhale the oxygen.

Students are taught to keep themselves safe as they help others. They must remember to use gloves, masks, and special eyewear. This is necessary to protect EMTs from getting infections.

Paramedics are trained to give certain lifesaving medicines to patients. ▼

Paramedic Training

Some EMTs go on to become paramedics. They must take 1,000 hours of training. This is in addition to EMT training. Paramedics are trained and licensed to do certain things that EMTs are not. For example, paramedics can give medicines to patients. They can give certain lifesaving medicines, such as nitroglycerin, to patients. This powerful drug helps to increase blood flow. It can help a patient live through a heart attack.

▲ A paramedic works
with doctors to save
a patient's life.

    As part of their training, paramedics work in hospitals. They
learn what it is like to treat real patients in an emergency. Doctors
act as coaches to help them learn to do their jobs. Paramedics often
talk with their assigned physicians when called to an emergency.
They use two-way radios to describe the scene and the patient's
condition. Paramedics and doctors can then decide on the best
treatment plan.

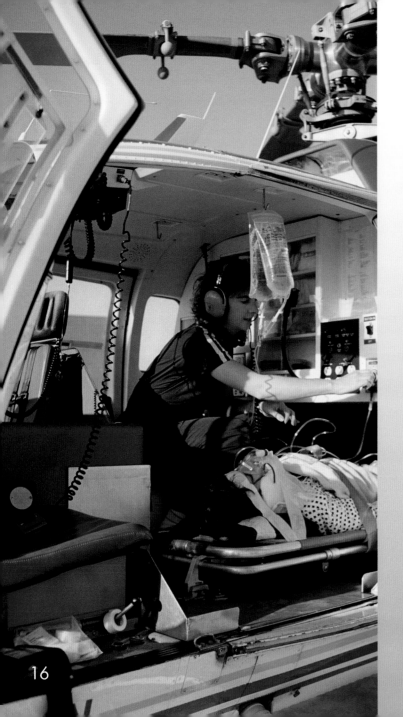

Advanced Life Support

Paramedic students learn to give Advanced Life Support (ALS). This is a type of medical aid. For example, they learn how to start an intravenous line (IV). An IV is a tube. It travels from a bag filled with saline (salt) solution or other fluid into a patient's arm. The solution enters the patient's arm through a needle. It acts like other fluids in the bloodstream. It can flow—like blood does—for a short period of time. This works until a patient can get to a hospital. IVs give a patient fluids when there is not enough water in the body. An IV can also put medicine directly into a patient's veins. This is important if he or she can't swallow pills.

Paramedic students need to learn how to treat many kinds of illnesses. They study medicines and medical testing machines. They are trained to use a cardiac (heart) machine that shows heart rhythms. Paramedics can tell if someone is having a heart attack by reading what the machine prints out.

◀ **A paramedic hooks a patient up to an IV.**

Keep Safe So You Won't Need to Call EMS

- Never play with matches.
- Wear a helmet and pads when you ride a bike, skateboard, or rollerskate.
- Stop, look, and listen before you cross the street.
- Don't approach dogs that you do not know well.
- Always wear your seat belt.

Calls to 911

Dispatchers are workers who make sure that calls to 911 are sent to the right people. Ambulance dispatchers handle calls to American Medical Response (AMR). They send out the ambulance crew closest to an emergency.

Dispatchers must stay calm. They decide how serious a call is. And they must send help to the right place quickly. Dispatchers tell ambulance crews where to go. They also tell them what kind of medical problem to expect. Life-threatening emergencies—such as heart attacks and car accidents—get ambulances before less serious emergencies.

A 911 dispatcher must send ▲ help to the right place quickly.

A computer shows different calls in progress—red is the most important. ▶

Dispatchers receive special training. They learn how to talk with people to find out what the problem is. This helps them understand which calls need immediate attention. They also receive training on special computer and phone systems.

Dispatchers ▶ receive special training on the phone system and computer used to handle 911 calls.

Paramedics stock the medicine bag for their ambulance.

On the Job

After students complete their training, they can become EMS volunteers. They can also work for private ambulance companies for pay. They will usually work in pairs.

An EMT checks the two-way radio to be sure it works.

Before going on a call, an EMT must make sure that the oxygen tanks are full. ▶

Each team must check supplies and equipment in their ambulance. They make sure they have everything they will need to do their jobs. EMTs check the AED machine. They also check the medical bags. These bags must have bandages, scissors, and IV bags. EMTs make sure that oxygen tanks are full and that they work.

Paramedics stock the medicine bag. They also check equipment, such as the nebulizer. This tool turns medicine into mist. Patients can inhale it through their mouths and noses. This helps people who have trouble swallowing get the medicine they need.

◀ An EMS worker rushes
to an emergency scene.

Help Is on the Way

EMS workers must know their neighborhoods
well. This way, they can quickly find their way
to any location. There is no time to waste
when an EMS team gets a call! A driver turns
on the ambulance's lights and sirens when
there is a life-and-death emergency. Out of
1,000 emergency calls, though, only about
200 require lights and sirens.

Turning on the lights and sirens—
only 200 out of 1,000 calls
require them. ▲

It is important for ▲ EMS workers to know their neighborhoods well so they can quickly get to a scene.

Arriving on the Scene

EMS workers must be in good shape. They often need to carry heavy equipment up stairs. They carry oxygen and a medical bag. They also have to carry patients to the ambulance.

EMS workers must be in good shape to carry their equipment up stairs and patients to an ambulance ▼

24

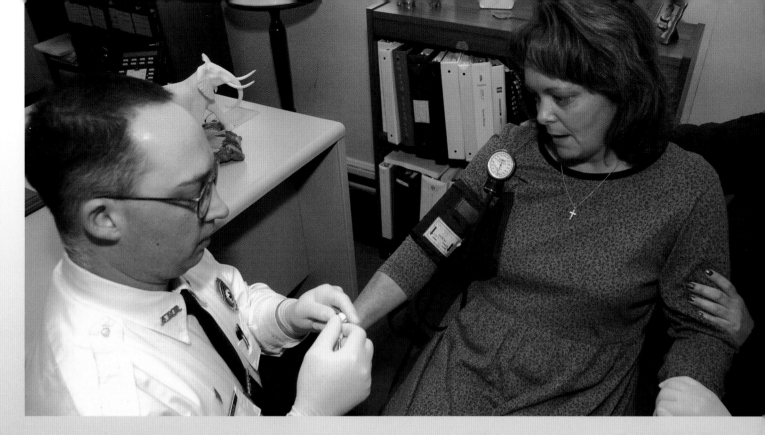

EMS teams quickly look over patients to see what is wrong. They check the person's heart rate and make sure that he or she is breathing. They can tell if a person is at risk of having a heart attack. If a person is unconscious or is not breathing, an EMS team begins CPR. If a patient is awake and alert, the team asks questions to find out what is wrong. They may ask about a patient's medical history. They will ask if he or she is taking medicines. They ask the patient what happened right before he or she felt sick.

Patients are often scared when they have a health emergency. EMS teams are specially trained to calm people who are upset.

Workers must carefully move their patients to an ambulance. ▲

Getting a Patient Out of Immediate Danger

EMTs and paramedics do whatever they can to get a patient out of immediate danger. For example, if a person has been in a car accident, EMS workers check the patient before moving him or her. They do this to tell if the patient has any broken bones or a neck injury. Moving a patient with a neck injury can make the problem worse. EMS workers must keep a patient's neck from moving while they carry him or her to the ambulance.

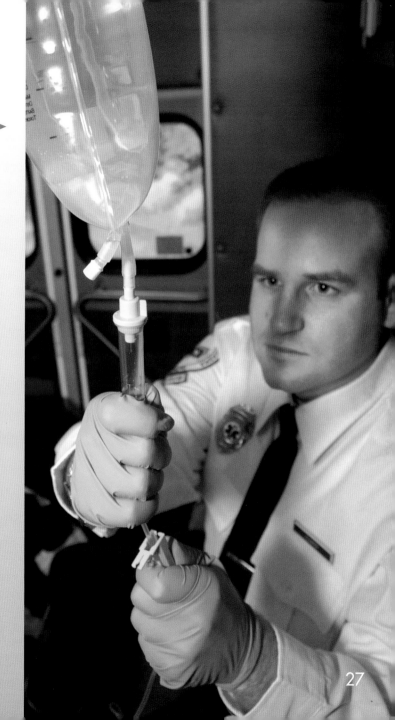

Sometimes a patient has another symptom while the EMS team is there. For example, a person who has had a heart attack may stop breathing. The team must pay attention. They continue to watch the patient as they treat him or her.

Teamwork is very important. Each EMS worker has an assigned job. For example, an EMT may give the patient oxygen. A paramedic may get an IV ready. EMS teams carefully carry patients to an ambulance once they can be moved. The team can use machines and other supplies kept inside the ambulance. For example, a paramedic can hook up patients to a heart monitor or give them medicine if necessary.

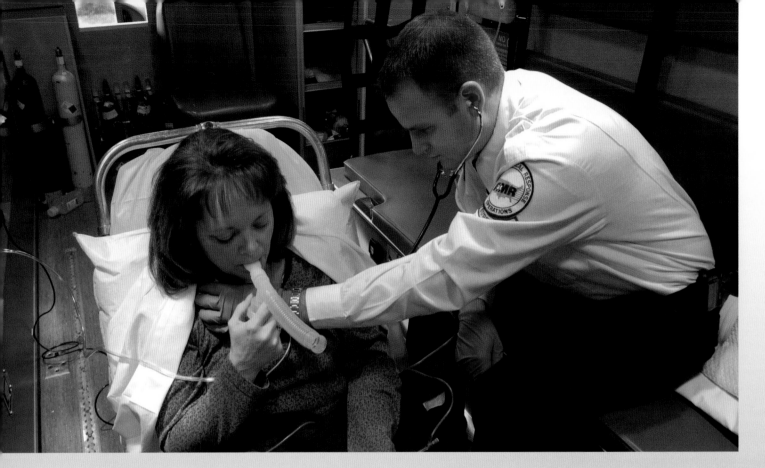

A patient may need ▲
help breathing on
the way.

Inside the Ambulance

EMS workers must take seriously ill patients to a hospital.
Here, doctors can decide if victims need more help. EMS
workers use the "golden nine minutes" rule. This means
that they try to have the patient on the way to the hospital
within nine minutes. Studies show that patients are more
likely to survive when they get to a hospital quickly.

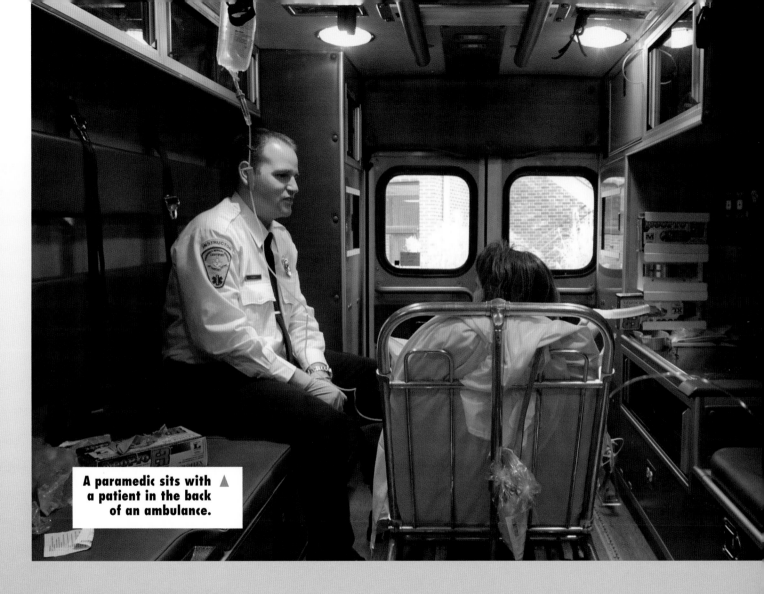

A paramedic sits with
a patient in the back
of an ambulance. ▲

EMS workers move patients safely in and out of an ambulance. One
EMS worker drives. The other worker watches patients on the ride to a hospital.

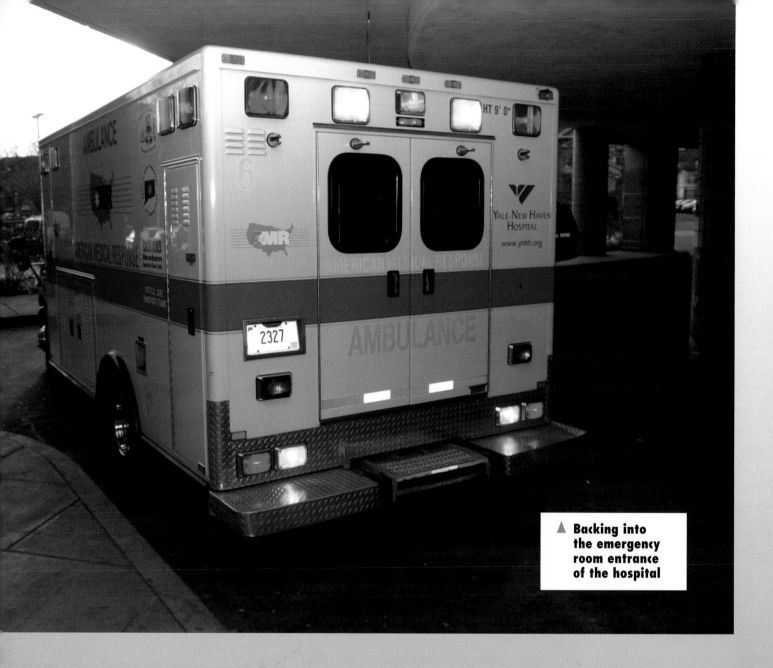

Backing into the emergency room entrance of the hospital

At the Hospital

At the hospital, an EMS team lifts patients onto a stretcher. They move the stretcher from outside of the ambulance to inside the emergency room. A nurse or doctor then takes over. EMS workers report what happened to the patient. They tell a doctor whatever they can about a patient. They explain what they've done for the person so far. At this point, an EMS worker's job is done. And it's time to wait for the next call!

EMS workers lift a patient onto a stretcher.

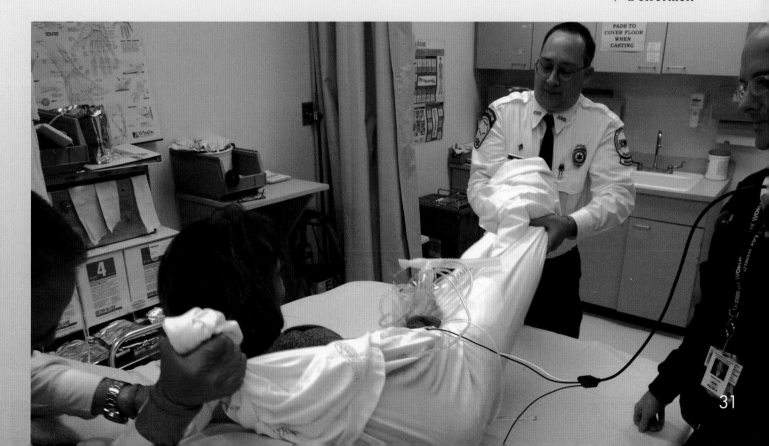

31

Glossary

AED Automatic External Defibrillator. Used to shock the heart into beating normally during a heart attack

Cardiac Heart related

CPR Cardiopulmonary Resuscitation. A technique used to get the heart and lungs to work properly after a trauma

EMS Emergency Medical Services

Heart Machine Used to see the rhythm of a person's heart

Nebulizer A tool that turns medicine into a mist

Nitroglycerin A drug that can help a person during a heart attack

Paramedic A licensed professional EMS worker who works under a physician to help patients during emergencies

For More Information

The American Ambulance Association

   www.the-aaa.org

National Highway Traffic Safety Administration

   www.nhtsa.org

American Medical Response

   www.amr-inc.com

Index

J616.02   Englart, Mindi Rose.
ENG
          EMS worker.

$24.94

DATE			
OCT 1 2			
SEP 2 6 2007